JAMES WARHOLA

Uncle Andy's

PUFFIN BOOKS

for
Dad and Mom

PUFFIN BOOKS
Published by the Penguin Group
Penguin Young Readers Group, 345 Hudson Street, New York, New York 10014, U.S.A.
Penguin Group (Canada), 10 Alcorn Avenue, Toronto, Ontario, Canada M4V 3B2
(a division of Pearson Penguin Canada Inc.)
Penguin Books Ltd, 80 Strand, London WC2R 0RL, England
Penguin Ireland, 25 St Stephen's Green, Dublin 2, Ireland (a division of Penguin Books Ltd)
Penguin Group (Australia), 250 Camberwell Road, Camberwell, Victoria 3124, Australia
(a division of Pearson Australia Group Pty Ltd)
Penguin Books India Pvt Ltd, 11 Community Centre, Panchsheel Park, New Delhi - 110 017, India
Penguin Group (NZ), Cnr Airborne and Rosedale Roads, Albany, Auckland,
New Zealand (a division of Pearson New Zealand Ltd)
Penguin Books (South Africa) (Pty) Ltd, 24 Sturdee Avenue, Rosebank, Johannesburg 2196, South Africa

Registered Offices: Penguin Books Ltd, 80 Strand, London WC2R 0RL, England

First published in the United States of America by G. P. Putnam's Sons,
a division of Penguin Putnam Books for Young Readers, 2003
Published by Puffin Books, a division of Penguin Young Readers Group, 2005

7 9 10 8

THE LIBRARY OF CONGRESS HAS CATALOGED THE PUTNAM EDITION AS FOLLOWS:
Warhola, James.
Uncle Andy's / James Warhola.
p. cm.
Summary: The author describes a trip to see his uncle, the soon-to-be-famous artist Andy Warhol,
and the fun that he and his family had on the visit.
ISBN: 0-399-23869-7
1. Warhol, Andy, 1928- –Juvenile literature. [1. Warhol, Andy, 1928- –Family.
2. Warhola, James—Childhood and youth. 3. Artists.]
I. Title.
N6537.W28 W375 2003 2002007766

Puffin Books ISBN 978-0-14-240347-1

Manufactured in China

Author's Note

Paul Warhola was the eldest of three brothers who grew up in the smoky industrial city of Pittsburgh. He and his wife, Ann, moved to the country to raise their seven children. He loved his junk business, which allowed him to be his own boss and choose his own hours. Life in the countryside was far from easy, but for us kids, we had a wonderful carefree existence.

Paul's youngest brother, Andy, left Pittsburgh for New York City in 1949 and soon dropped the *a* from his name to become known as Andy Warhol. He became very successful as a commercial illustrator. During the early 1960s Andy entered the realm of fine art. He was part of a small group of artists who believed that they could stretch the limits of art even more by portraying ordinary things that were popular to modern society. It quickly became known as pop art.

Every few months we made a pilgrimage to New York City to visit our Uncle Andy and our grandmother whom we affectionately referred to as Bubba (a Carpathian-Rusyn word meaning "grandmother"). As the trips progressed through the 1950s, there became more of us and our car acquired a caravan quality. As kids we looked forward to each trip as a great adventure to a very exotic land. A land apart from ours, where people dyed their hair purple and walked herds of dogs through the streets. Our oasis was Uncle Andy's and Bubba's house.

The following story is about a trip that we took in August of 1962. It was a very important year for Andy Warhol. He had his first solo exhibition, in which he introduced the world to his soup can paintings. Though he has achieved great prominence in the art world, we will always remember him as our Uncle Andy.

Paulie   Eva   MaryLou   Georgie   Jamie   Maddie   Marty

Looking back on those days, the one thing I remember most is thinking my dad had the best darn job in the world. Our yard was always so much more fun than anyone else's in the neighborhood. My oldest brother was already away at college, but there were still six of us at home. Dad had lots of jobs, but for now he was mostly a junkman. Sometimes the neighbors complained that our yard looked like a junkyard.

The real junkyard was about a mile away on a dirt road. It was up a really steep hill. It had everything—old cars, old pop machines, and old airplane engines. You name it. It was there on "The Hill." Dad's job was to take things apart and separate the metals—aluminum, copper, brass, and steel. When there was enough, he loaded the truck and hauled it to another junkyard.

Dad was always bringing home junk, and sometimes he'd say
to me, "Now, Jamie, this can really make good art." Then he'd
put a bunch of it together in an interesting way.

Mom was always yelling to Dad, "For Pete's sake, Paul, quit
junking up the house!" and "Paul, when you going to get rid of
this stuff, anyhow?" But we liked playing in the junk.

One day, Dad came home from work and announced, "It's time to visit Bubba and Uncle Andy in the big city. We'll leave tomorrow morning." Oh, we were so excited. It was not often that we got to visit our grandma and our famous artist uncle in New York City. We had a lot of getting ready to do.

Dad had work to do on the car. Mary Lou and Eva had to make sandwiches. Georgie and I had to pack the car, and little Maddie and Marty, well, they didn't do much, they were just in the way.

The next morning, Mom woke us up extra early and we were finally on our way. We saw nothing but cornfields and cow pastures at first. Then, we slowly counted the seven tunnels that it would take us to get there. When we came to the last tunnel, we all perked up.

All of a sudden the world became very different. There were giant buildings, honking taxis, and people going every which way. Dad slowly wove his way uptown to Uncle Andy's.

There we were, all eight of us standing in front of a huge black door, ringing the bell. After a long wait, the door unlatched and slowly opened. Uncle Andy peered out for a minute and then let out a long "Ohhhhh!" Dad always thought it was best not to phone ahead so that it would be a surprise. It certainly worked. Uncle Andy was always very, very surprised. He showed us in and we made our way to the kitchen, where our grandmother was.

Bubba drowned us with wet kisses as she always did and fixed us a dinner of salamis, breads, and cheeses. Soon all the chattering and eating came to an end and it was time for sleep. Uncle Andy showed us to our makeshift beds. I slept on the top floor on a propped-up old door covered with cushions.

In the morning, I noticed that I was surrounded by towers of soup boxes. I thought Uncle Andy and Bubba sure ate a lot of soup! But that wasn't it at all. Uncle Andy didn't buy those soup boxes, he built them out of wood and painted each one. They were art and really important too, because Uncle Andy told us not to touch any of it.

Dad always remembered to bring Uncle Andy something interesting from the junkyard. This time it was a giant magnet with a bunch of bolts stuck to it. Uncle Andy peered over his glasses at it real carefully, and after a pause he said, "Ohhh, gee. Wow!" Then we really knew he liked it. He decided that it should go right by the front door.

Uncle Andy had twenty-five cats, all named Sam. They were always hiding in a house that was just like a giant amusement park. It was perfect for hide-and-go-seek and racing. It wasn't long before the six of us were flying up and down the stairs and through all the rooms like a band of wild monkeys.

Uncle Andy thought everything
was art in some way or another.
That's why his house was so
fantastic. Each of the rooms
was filled to the brim with
all sorts of neat things.

There were always new things to see. Right
in the middle of the entranceway there was a
giant piece of crumpled metal. It looked like
it might have gotten stuck there and couldn't
go any farther. Uncle Andy explained to us,
"Oh, that's a piece of *faabbbulous*
art by a famous artist." We were
impressed. Dad had a lot
of that back home.

Uncle Andy was always making art. We loved watching him paint in his studio.
He made regular stuff like soup cans, pop bottles, and money look like real art!

Mary Lou and Eva just loved his giant pictures of Elvis Presley.
Mom, always aware of unnecessary clutter, asked, "Gee, Andy,
when you going to get rid of this stuff?"

Uncle Andy, startled, said, "Ohhh, no. This is art. It's going to
be worth a lot of money!" Mom really didn't understand art.

With all of the commotion that we caused, Uncle Andy decided it might be better to put us all to work. It wasn't long before each of us had different jobs. He knew I liked to do art, so he let me help him with his giant paint-by-number sailboat painting.

At night Uncle Andy went out to parties to see other famous people. In the morning, we patiently sat by his door, waiting for it to open so he could tell us all about who he had met. Once Maddie surprised Uncle Andy by going into his room a little too early. He let out a shriek because he didn't have his wig on yet!

Of course, we all knew Uncle Andy was bald, just like Dad and Uncle John. Uncle Andy had wigs for every occasion—messy wake-up wigs, multicolored afternoon wigs, and formal wigs for parties. He had given Dad his old wigs, and back at home we had a lot of fun with them.

Each day was a chance to see something new. We especially loved hiding in the studio when Uncle Andy had important art people over to talk about his work. They would all huddle around the paintings, pointing and peering. They really thought Uncle Andy was on to something. I knew his paintings were super neat and it made me want to do my own art when I got home.

Finally Dad announced, "It's time to get on home!" That night we packed up all of our things. Again, Mary Lou and Eva made the sandwiches. Bubba added a few salamis.

Uncle Andy was on his way out the door with one of his soup-can paintings when I told him we had to leave in the morning. He replied, "Ohhh, oh really? I have to go out to sell this picture to a man waiting at the corner. You know, he's the Taxicab King. He really likes my work. Then I'm going to a party. Ohhh, so have a *faabbbulous* trip, Jamie, bye."

We went to bed early, and before I knew it, Mom was wiggling my toes and saying, "Time to get up." Bubba helped us with our things and we trudged out into the dark morning. At the foot of the steps there were a bunch of boxes that Uncle Andy had left for all of us. A lot of neat stuff, including art supplies for me! Bubba drowned us with those wet kisses as we got into the car. Soon we were weaving our way downtown to go through the first tunnel. We all fell asleep wondering about our next trip back to Uncle Andy's.

As we got older, we made many more trips back to that faraway city and Dad continued bringing interesting junk from the junkyard for Uncle Andy. I really liked doing art, and I learned that art is something that is all around us all of the time.

In the corner of my bedroom, I made an art studio
of my own and although Mom fretted and fussed
as usual over what a mess it all was, she
didn't make me clean it up. She even woke
me up early on Saturdays to drive me to art class.
You know, I think Mom's finally understanding
what art is all about.